[illegible] published 2008 by Walker Books Ltd
[illegible] London SE11 5HJ

[illegible]

[illegible] Cataloguing in Publication Data is available [illegible]

YES NO

Jan Pieńkowski

yes

no

fast

slow

asleep

awake

alive

dead

in

out

over

off

on

light

heavy

old

up

down

before

after

left

right